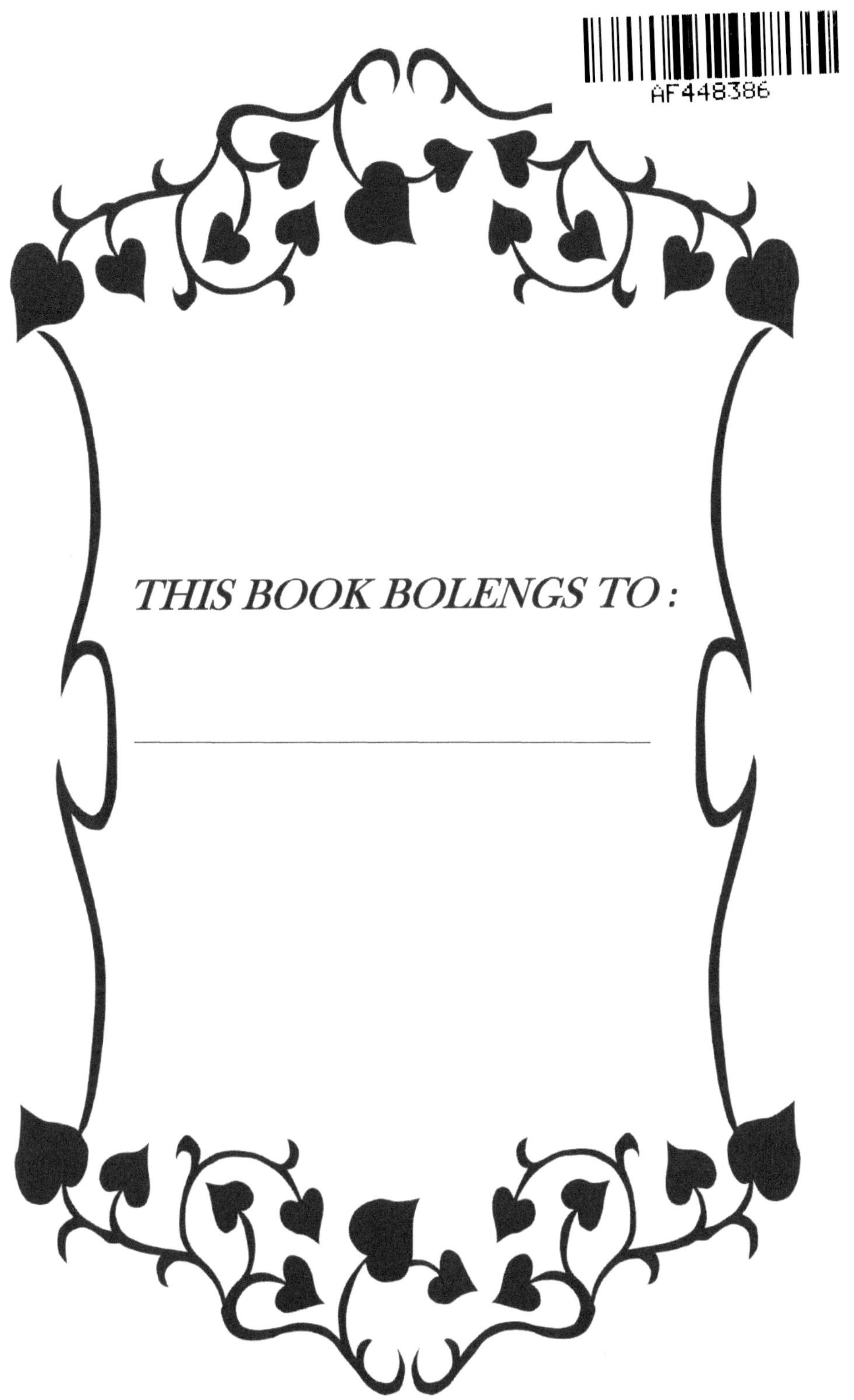

AF448386
THIS BOOK BOLENGS TO :

NUMBERS
1 2 3

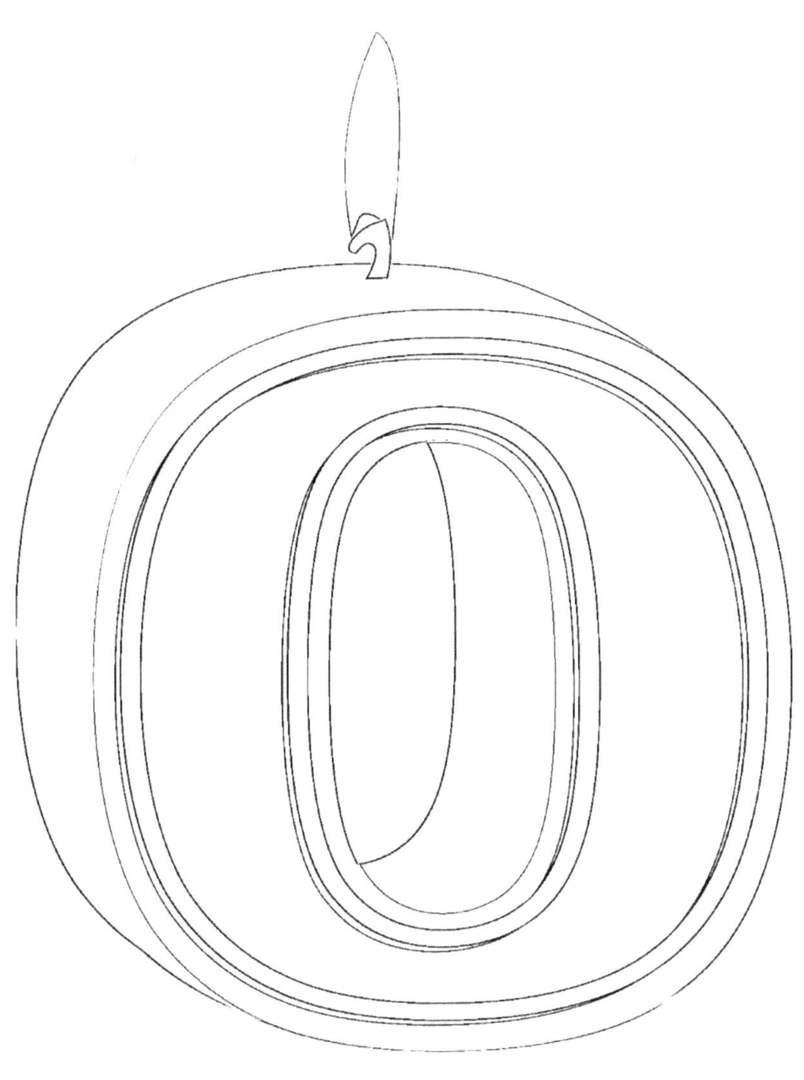

0

ZERO

1

ONE

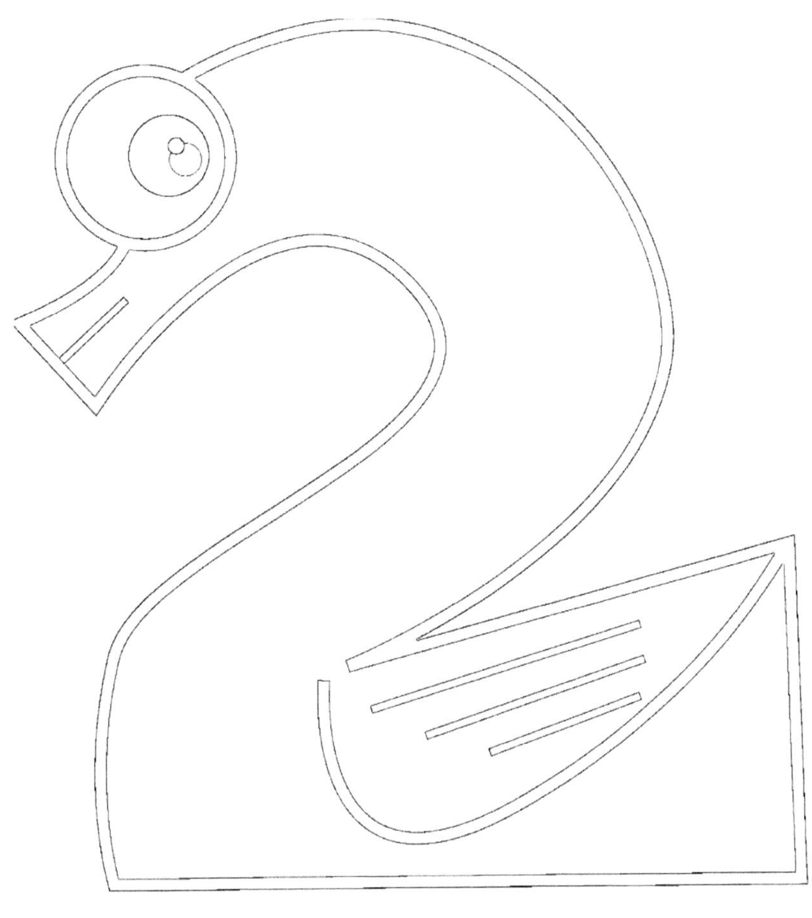

2

TOW

3

THREE

4

FOUR

5

FIVE

6

SIXE

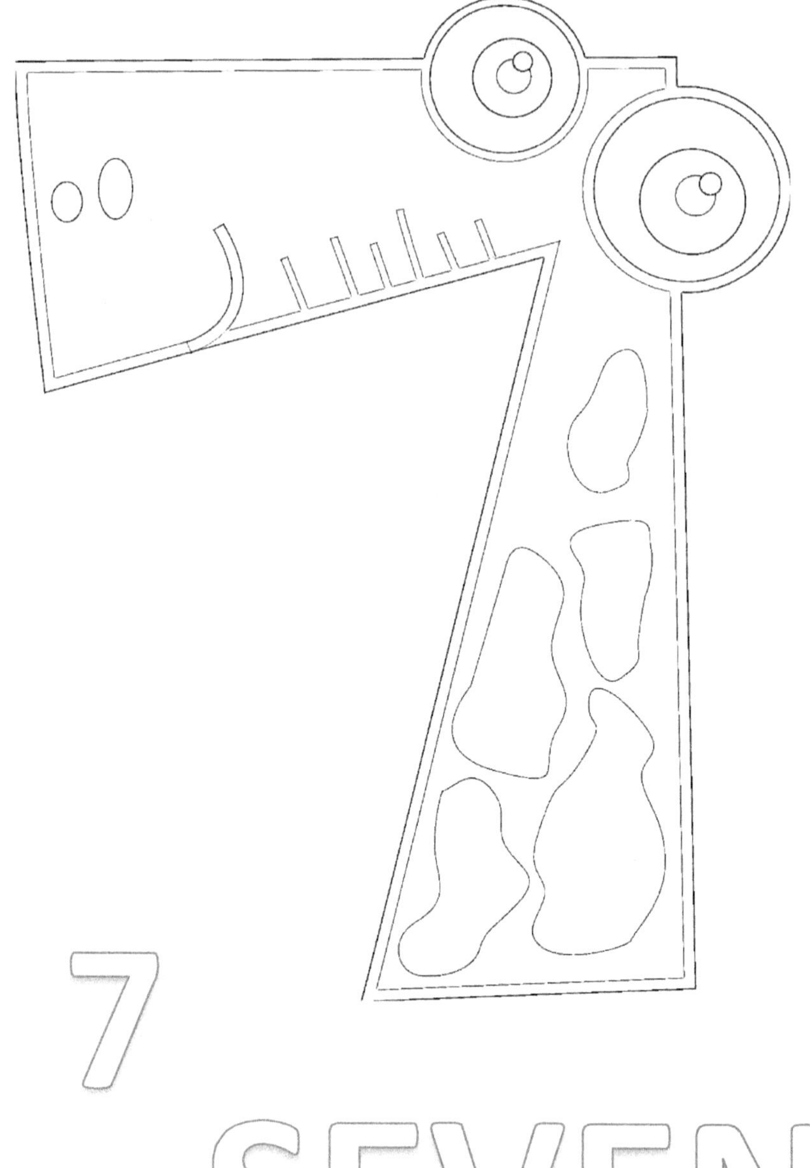

7

SEVEN

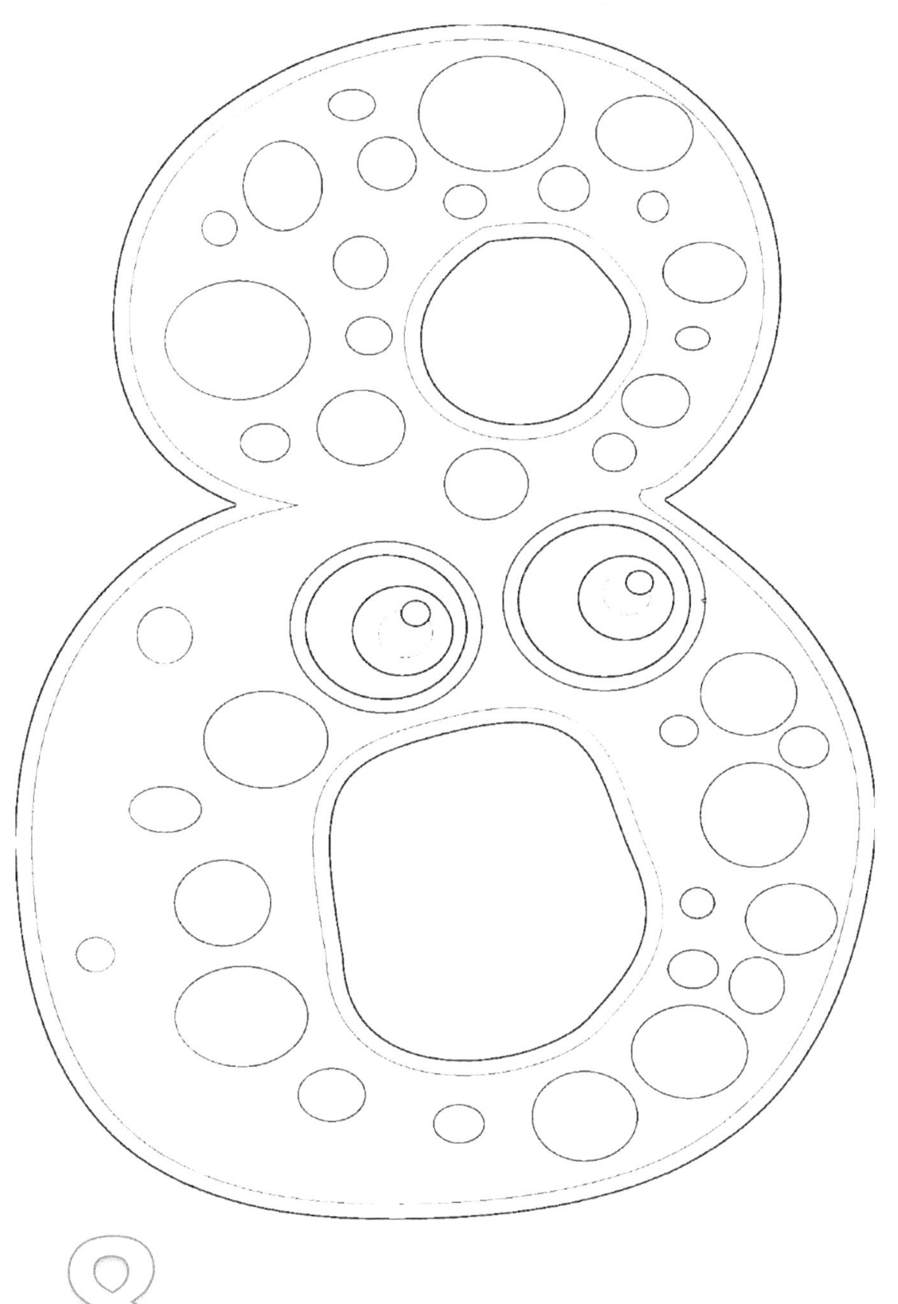

8

EIGHT

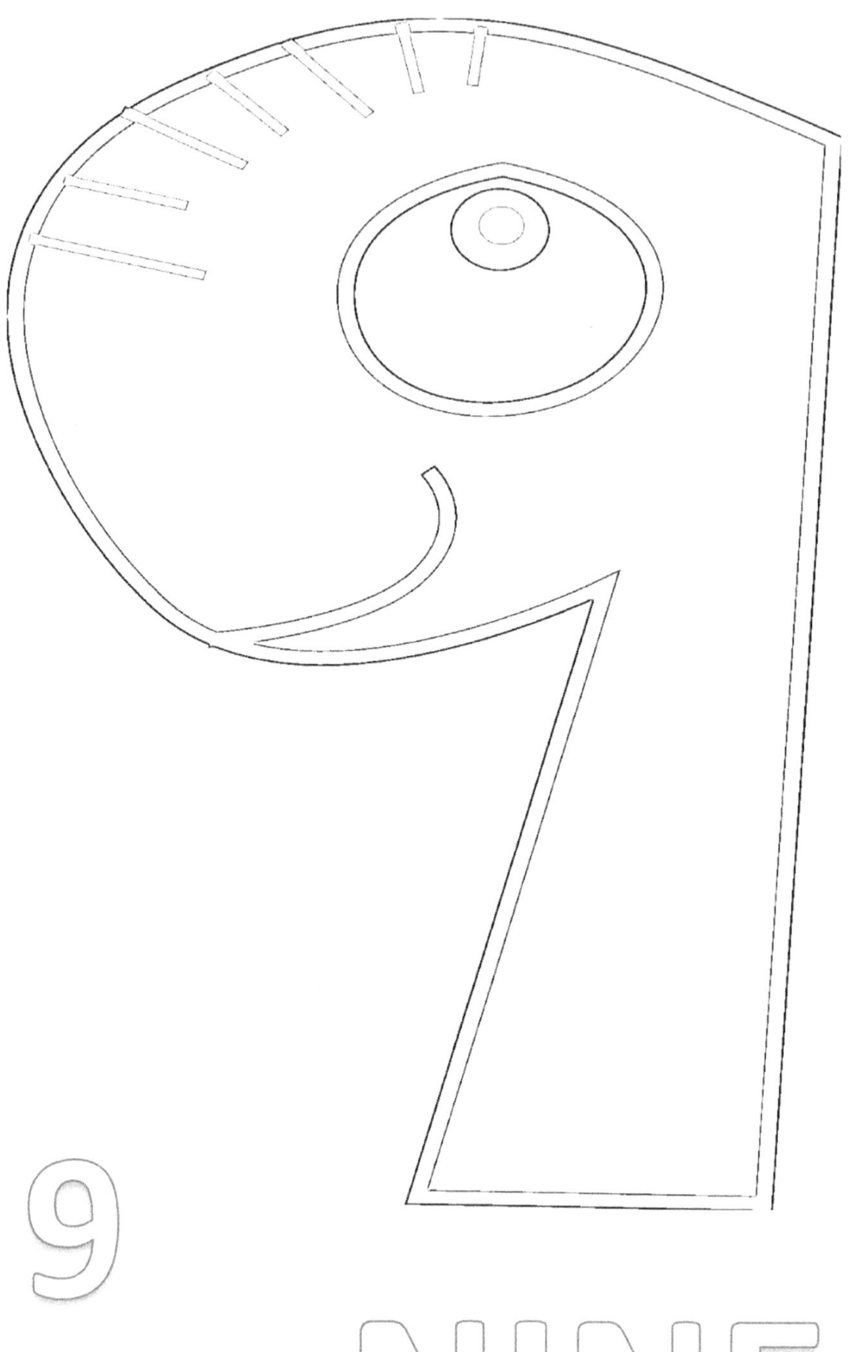

9

NINE

10

TEN

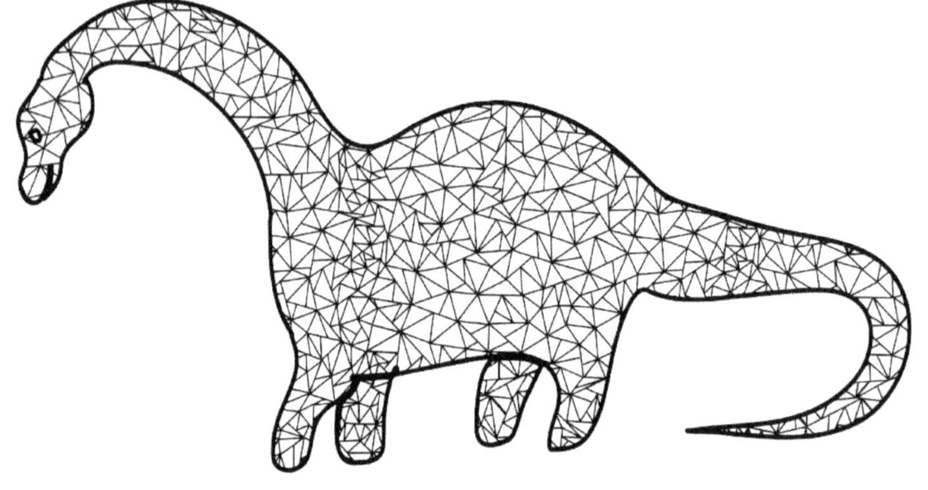

1

ONE

2 TOW

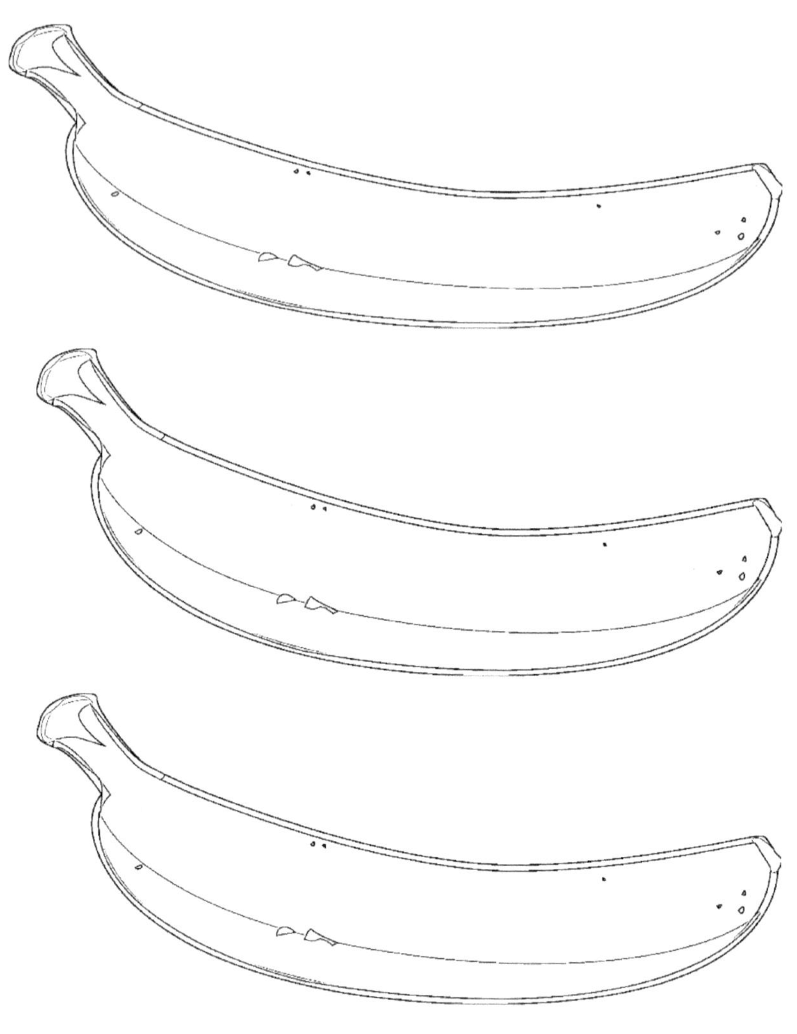

3 THREE

4

FOUR

5
FIVE

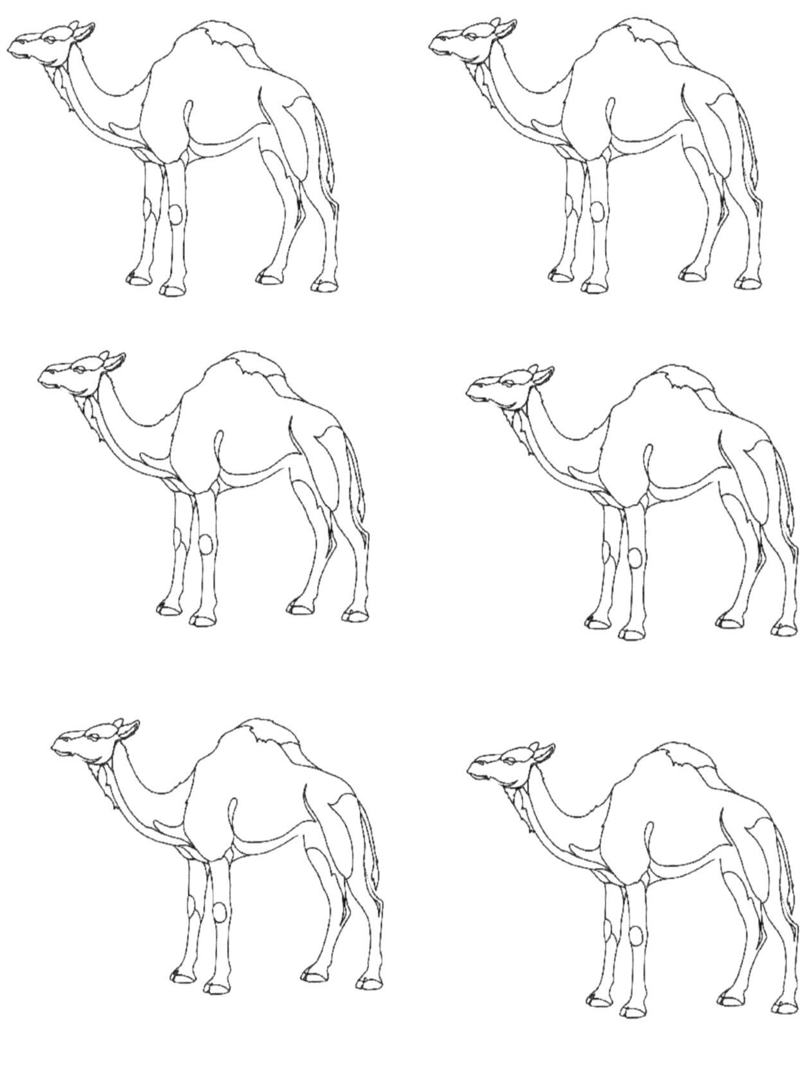

6 SIXE

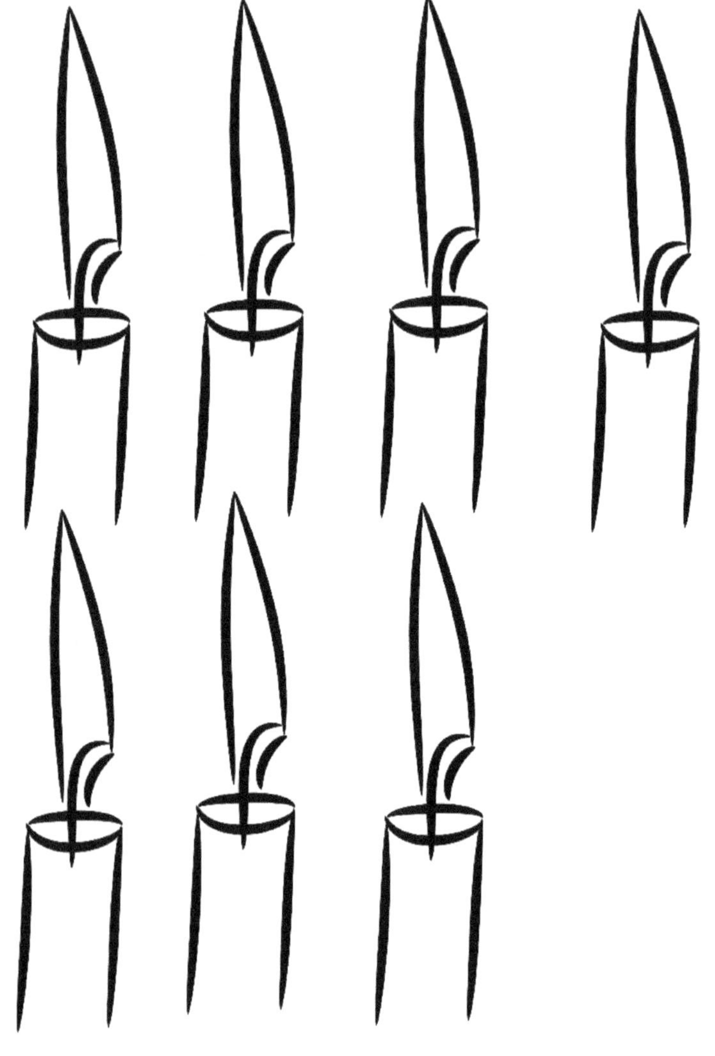

7 seven

8

EIGHT

9 NINE

10

TEN

LETTERS
A.B.C

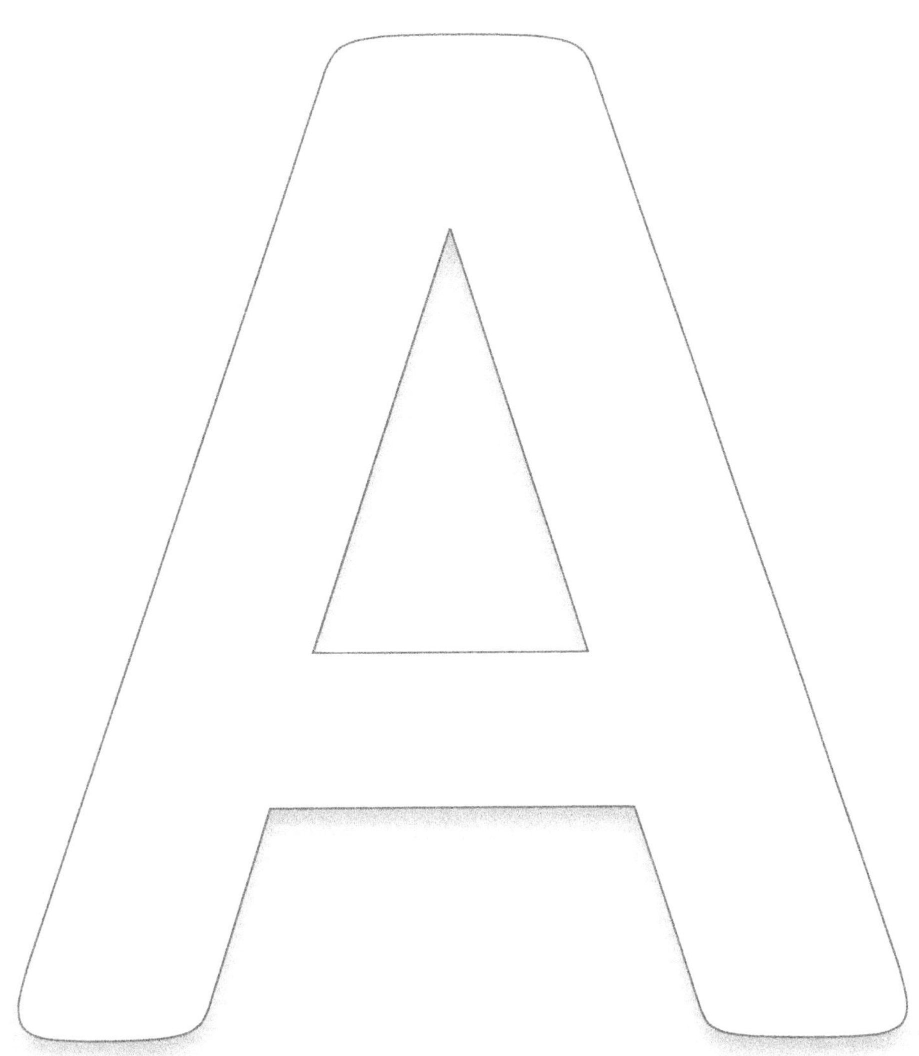

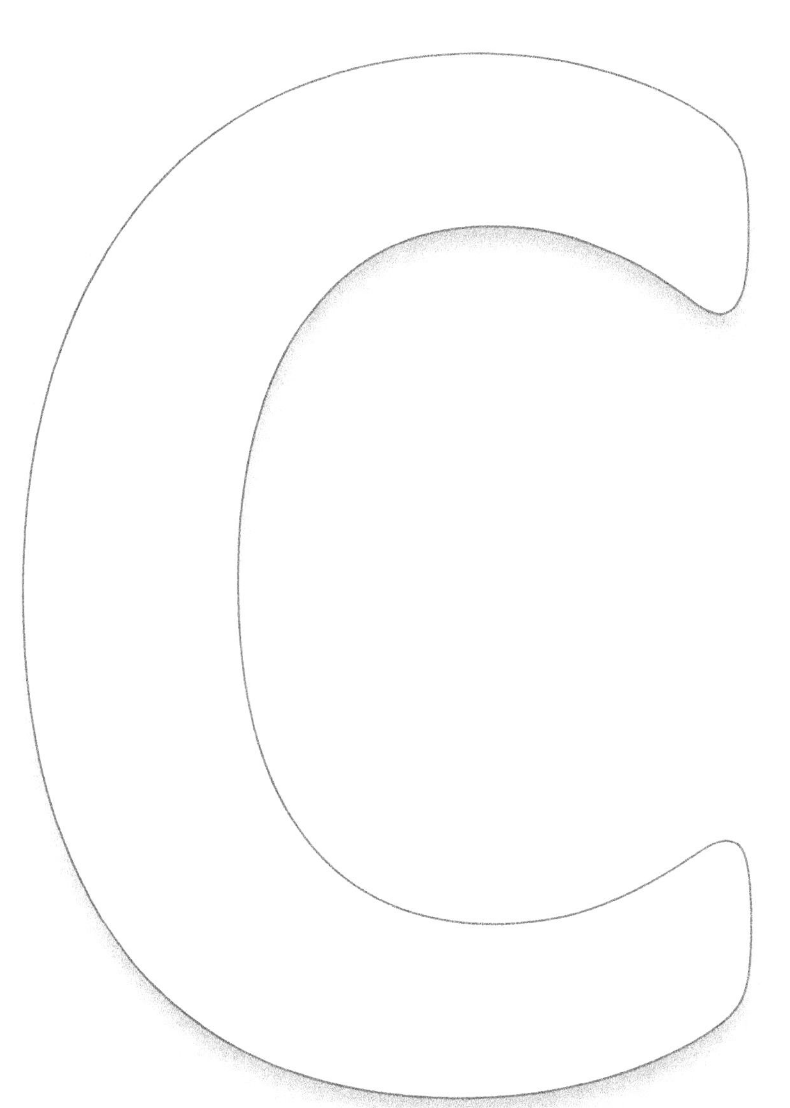

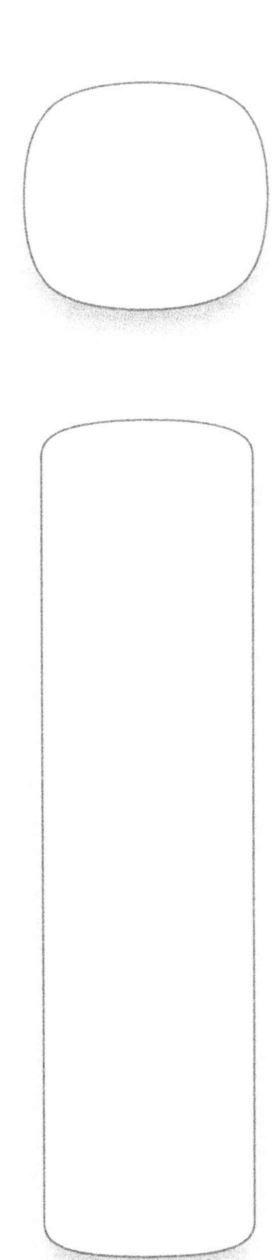

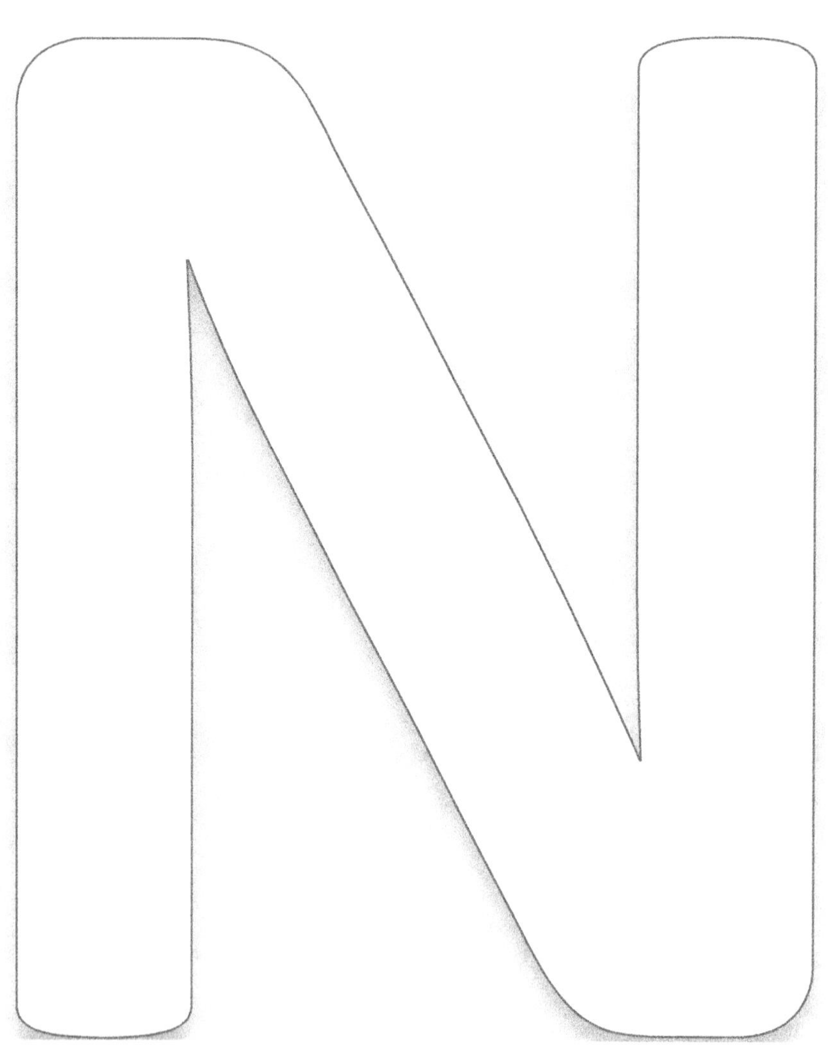

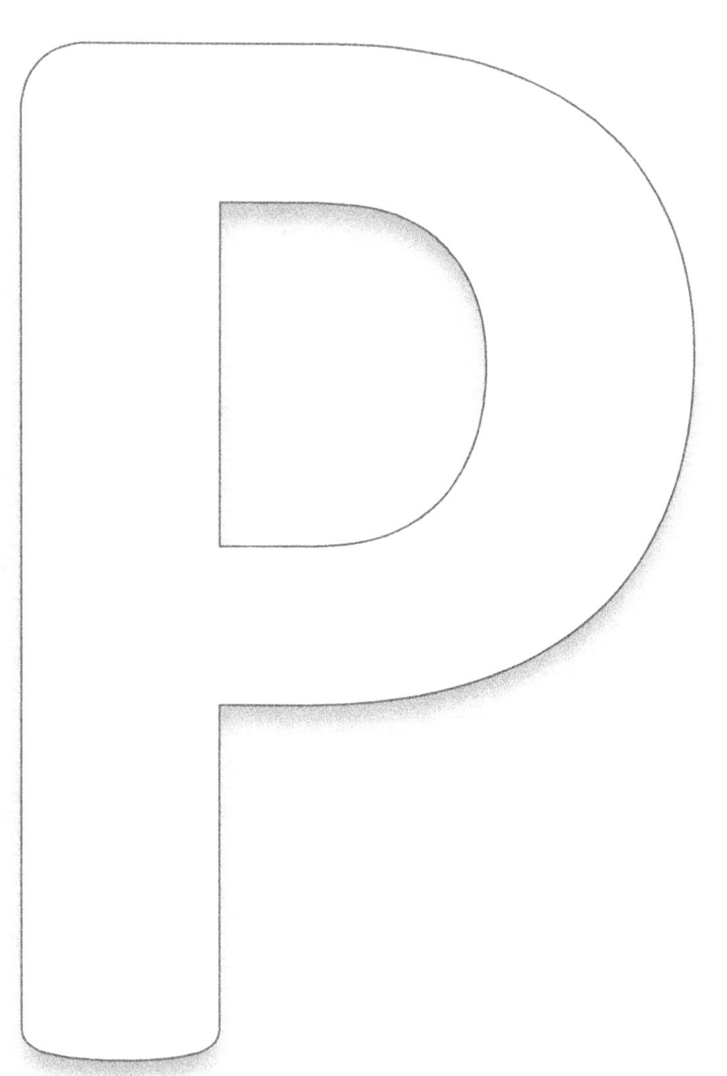

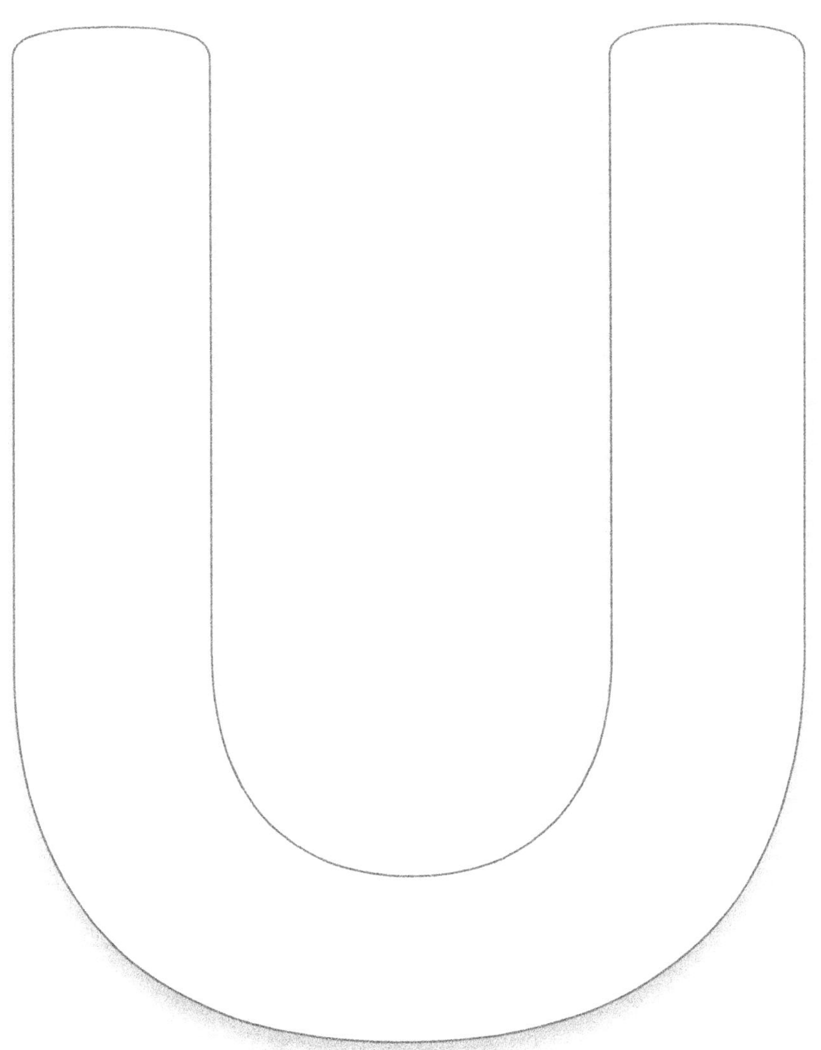

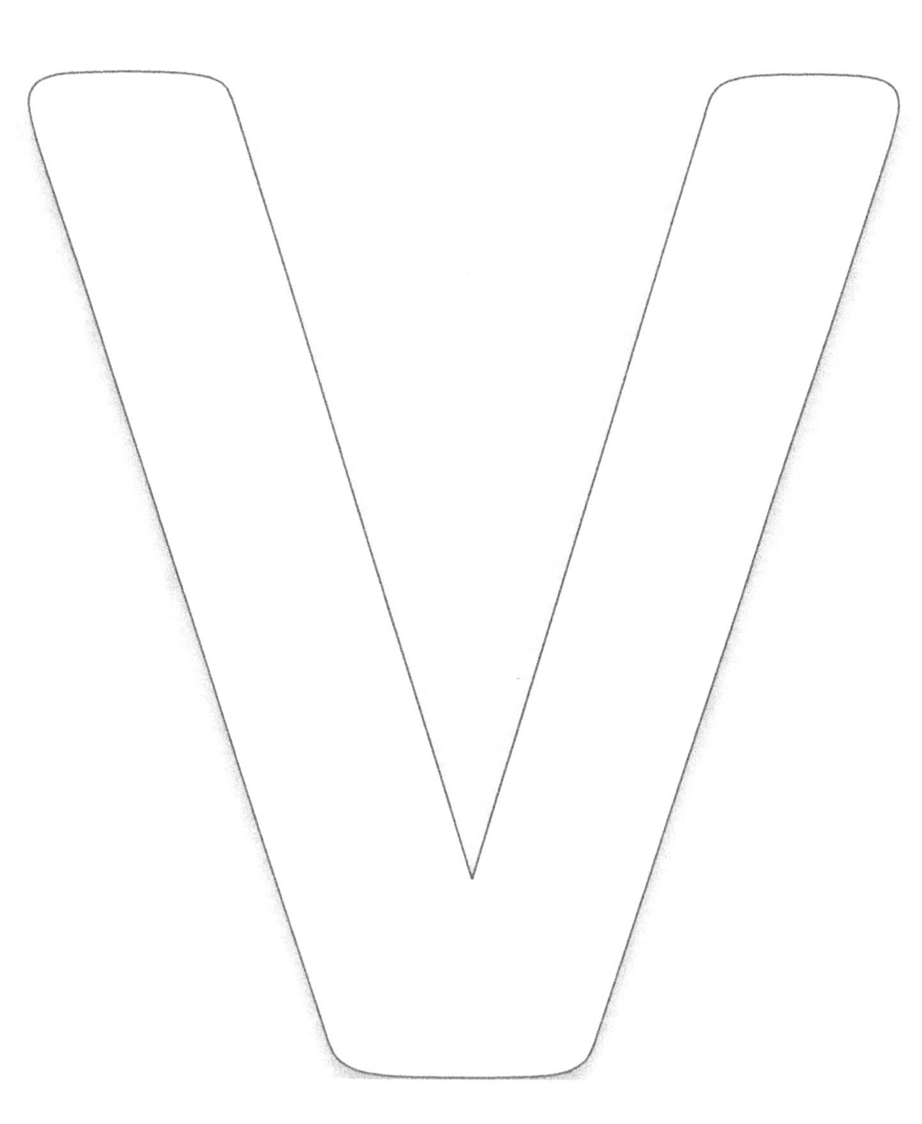

THE

END